MW01231903

1

Copyright page

_____

Darilyn Johnson

The Chapter's of Her

Darilyn Johnson

Table of Contents

Dedication

This book is dedicated to my children. You've seen your mother rise above heartache and yet still embrace and walk in God's favor. Your grandparents taught me survival and faith in part. As your mother I now teach and leave behind a legacy full of resources. I now teach you both survival and faith go together as *one*. My children, remember it's never too late to start over.

To the past that shaped me, the present that nurtures me, and the future that awaits me. For all the yesterdays that led me to today. To tomorrow, for it holds unspoken stories. For every moment that brought me to this point. To the time when this book was just a dream. To you, dear reader, for making this journey worthwhile. For my readers, who breathe life into these pages. To all those who pick up this book, thank you for giving my words a chance. For every reader who finds a piece of themselves within these chapters. To those reading this, may you find the courage, joy, and love contained within these pages. To the resilience of the human spirit, a beacon in the darkest storms. For those who rise from the ashes, time and time again. To the undying spark within us that keeps us going against all odds. For the human spirit that thrives on love, hope, and kindness. To the resilience of humanity, our greatest testament. This is dedicated to *you*.

Foreword

It is with profound honor and deep gratitude that I pen this foreword for Darilyn Johnson, a remarkable woman of faith, vision, and unwavering commitment to the empowerment of others. Darilyn, a successful healthcare guru and esteemed Prophetess, has dedicated her life to guiding women on a transformative journey to embrace their true selves, as seen through the eyes of God. Her latest work, "The Chapter's of Her: Empowering Women to Be Their True Self Through God's Path and Eyes" is a testament to her passion and divine calling.

Darilyn's journey was nothing short of inspiring. Her extensive experience in healthcare, coupled with her spiritual wisdom, uniquely positions her to understand the intricate connections between physical well-being, mental health, and spiritual fulfillment. Through her profound insights and practical guidance, she offers women a holistic approach to self-discovery and empowerment, free from the constraints of societal expectations and external influences. Her message is clear: true empowerment comes from aligning oneself with God's vision and purpose.

In this book, Darilyn masterfully weaves together personal anecdotes, and actionable advice to create a roadmap for women seeking to live authentically and purposefully. Her words resonate with compassion, strength, and divine wisdom, offering readers not just inspiration, but a tangible path to transformation. As you delve into this book, I encourage you to open your heart and mind to Darilyn's teachings. May her words illuminate your path, strengthen your faith, and empower you to become the woman God has always intended you to be.

With blessings and admiration,

Prophet Jeremy Butler

Preface

Realizing that you are "Her" requires you to discover what it took for you to become. It looks like visiting all the places you left behind, remembering your roots and self-discovery. As we journey through how I became *HER* it is my ultimate goal to show you that you are capable of holding that same confidence in your hands. You are capable of owning your story in a way that impacts lives forever, too. So what if you've bumped your head along the way, so did your favorite influencer, childhood hero, favorite preacher and everyone else God put on this earth. Becoming Her means not letting people tell you who "Her" is. Becoming Her means you write your own story and narrative with the help of God. It is accepting that you have more power to affirm yourself in ways the world never did. "That's *HER*" is always how people have referred to me. It's always how others took it upon themselves to describe me or share a story about me, both good and bad. I got to a point in womanhood where I had become okay with being "Her" as long as I defined it! One thing about my story, is that I own the rights to it. When I truly grabbed ahold of my authority and realized the power in that, everything shifted.

I'M *HER* the woman that delayed her own advancement. A woman that took shortcuts only to end up going back the long way. I'M *HER*, who had two children and never got married. I'M *HER* who built a man up and put myself second. I'M *HER* who postponed her own educational goals to live a life of "outside." I'M *HER* who ran from ministry because I didn't know how to balance purpose and business. I'M *HER* who has poured into people on empty. I'M *HER* who has had the taste for things that added no value to my future.

As Her, I won't stop fulfilling what that truly means. Day by day, moment by moment and chapter by chapter I discover more of Her. I invite "Her" in, I challenge Her, I love Her and I go after "Her" with everything in me! I'm *HER* and who that is, is subject to get better and better, subject to heal, subject to live life loud and whole and subject to impact lives around this country. I invite you to become *HER*, too.

Chapter One

I'm Her

I was A little girl from Fort Worth, Texas

who desired to be a criminal attorney for the
city. I remember as a little girl in my parents
living room pretending I was a lawyer in a court
room just to then shift like I was conducting my
own church service. Even though I was only
pretending I would walk in such authority as a
little girl. I had a certain determination that told
me I was born for these things before I even
fully understood what they were. I was born
with a big personality. I was born to be

independent, outspoken, and to own the rooms I entered. Unknowingly, I was a threat to many so I stayed guarded yet outspoken. I was raised to never let your right hand know what your left is doing. I was determined, consistent and observing.

I grew up in a very close family. Even if we had an issue going on we were good at covering one another. From the outside looking in you would never know it was any animosity. We protected our name, and that stuck with me forever. I was a daddy's girl through and through. I have one sister, and one brother both older than I am. I'm the only girl on my mother's side of the family, so growing up strength was no option. In my family, I had two different worlds. My mother's parents are the ones who instilled the survival piece in me. They made sure we secured us, then everyone else. They stood firm in that. They attended church, they were Baptist but it wasn't the same as my father's side. My dad's side was a mix of both flashy and faith.

Before my parents split, I grew up in a very structured family and household. There was always a standard set that one must abide by and that continued even after their split. They were united when it came to parenting. Though my parents did not stay together, they had a solid co-parenting method that didn't leave me falling through the cracks. My parents were almost polar opposites as far as their paths. My father taught me faith, but my mother taught me survival. My father was a Pastor and Prophet of a Non-Denominational church while my mother worked as a machine warehouse worker for thirty-two years. Though their lives were so different, I learned commitment to my own path, from them both.

My mother and father split when I was five years old due to my mom realizing what she wanted in life was just different. She had no desire to be a first Lady of a church and when she became clear on that, she stood by her decision regardless of her love for my father. This decision was written in permanent ink and it taught me to stand on my own very early. Because of this, very early in age, I recognized that women had choices and later on in life I would face many choices of my own. This would be the example of what deciding looked like. Knowing this was my mother's decision left me somewhere in the middle of if ministry was for me or if I would follow in her foot steps and live a life without the mantle. Despite my thoughts, I recognized, that the Lord had called me to ministry and though I would try to compromise or dodge the call, I would eventually completely surrender.

I remember as a little girl in my parents living room pretending like I was conducting my own church service then I would shift to pretending I was a Lawyer in a courtroom. Part of my pretending would include walking in such authority as a little girl. My parents knew in their hearts that I was destined for great things. Even as a young girl I was gifted. My parents could see it so clearly. I was groomed for ministry on my father's side while my mother's side was grooming me for success as an attorney. Regardless of what I was to become, they knew it would be great. When I was very young my father would call me "Prophetess". He saw my gift and he spoke it over me very young. With my mother being Baptist, all of that was extra in her opinion as it just wasn't apart of the church she was used to. She raised me to be a believer and to go to church, but that is where it started and stopped. In general she was a lot more practical, much like her parents, so that looked like college and a successful career to sustain me.

At age seventeen I graduated early from high school with a full ride to Stephen F. Austin college. The minute I graduated I was *free*. *Free* to live this life with no boundaries. I was *free* to finally discover the twin in me that wanted what the world wanted. That looked like freedom, sex, money, and the wild side. College didn't line up with that side of me. It would take that determination factor I had since I was a little girl. The standard my parents set before me was revealing itself once again. Here I was, having to decide to follow my own heart or follow the standard in front of me. There was only one choice for me to make.

I remember when I decided not to take the scholarship and go off to school. It was the week I was set to leave. My parents had already bought everything I needed to go, all the way down to my dorm room necessities. I gave my mother the excuse that I just didn't want to leave her, and though it was true, it was much more than that. I quickly decided I would attend a local college. My parents were disappointed because they knew there was more in store for me. They all believed that I was gonna live out my childhood dream, and be an Attorney. They felt that this was a wasted opportunity and money down the drain. Apart of me knew she was right and apart of me knew, I had to make the decision anyway. The thing is, some things we must learn, whether it is from love or from life.

It was unbelievable how hard it was for me to run. Men use to tell me all the time "You are different I can't touch or talk to you." I use to hear this so much that it began to scare me. My gift followed me. Even while I was trying to explore my wild side, who I was called to be, was always seen. The hand of God was all over me and I couldn't run from it. I may as well have walked around with a sign on my head that said "The Pastors daughter". I had no problem with being the Pastors daughter, but I was at a point in my life where I wanted to know more about what it meant to be Darilyn. I wanted to explore the other side of the standard my parents set, like all women coming of age do. I had no idea what was ahead of me, but the more uncertain I was the more I longed for it.

When I began college I met a man that turned out to be a father of one of my children. After class I went to grab some food at KFC when I met him in the drive-through. Before handing

21

me my food the words "You gone be my baby mama one day!" came flying out his mouth. This boy had lost his mind. There was no way the man in the drive-through giving me my food, was gonna get me pregnant. Who knew that I wouldn't just end up eating KFC but I'd be eating those words. Exactly two months later we met in a different setting and the rest was history. I liked him so much, you couldn't tell me nothing about that man. I stopped going to school after one year of being with him and we spent all of our time together. We were inseparable. Often times I wonder what life would be like had I stayed the course. Instead life took a slow but exciting turn.

He and I were together for five years before I became pregnant with our beautiful daughter. He was a respectful guy who treated me nicely. All of the things I didn't appreciate in our relationship, were replaced with potential. After a while I had to realize I was settling for potential, with no proof. Yeah, he was a good guy but he wasn't checking all of the boxes and that became abundantly clear throughout my pregnancy. I was footing the bill far too often, and I was about to have a child who needed me. I was constantly considering the fact that he just wasn't bringing enough to the table but I wasn't doing anything about it. We had a beautiful connection but even after five years, we just weren't on the same path.

My entire pregnancy was spiritual. Amidst all the other things, it was during the nine of months of my pregnancy my prophetic gifting started to get stronger. Isn't it funny how the Lord will keep you even when you do not want to be kept? I would see so many things in the spirit while pregnant. As you may know, the prophetic is often to warn us and that's exactly what it did for me during pregnancy. During the end of my pregnancy I would dream and see telephone numbers. Finally, one night in my dream I saw a number and I felt the need to call it. I then began to dream about this woman that my then boyfriend (and father of my child) was cheating with! Finally, I decided to call the number I dreamed. I knew it had to be *hers*. I called the woman and I asked her for the truth, she told me there was no way she was sleeping with my boyfriend but I didn't believe her. After hanging up the phone I got out of the bed, nine months pregnant and all and I drove to his house and there she was, walking out of his door.

Two weeks prior to having my daughter she stopped moving. I saw in the spirit that something was wrong but doctors couldn't confirm it because the baby had a heartbeat. We had no idea why this happened but what I did know was, I wasn't off, they were. During labor they finally saw what I knew all along in my heart, something was wrong. She wasn't moving because the umbilical cord was wrapped around her neck so tightly. The doctor couldn't even loosen it with his fingers between the cord and her neck. He needed her to shift. I was in labor with my babygirl for over twenty-four hours. The stress on labor caused my body to go into literal shock. The look on everyone's faces in the room was something I still to this day can't explain. Everyone in the room begin to panic and my child was in distress.

It was my daughter's grandmother who told the doctors to clear the room and she would take it from there. She wasn't a registered nurse nor a doctor but when a black woman speaks, you hear power and you abide. We were racing against the clock, time nor circumstance was on our side, but

God was. I had no more energy to push. I was truly relying on the strength of God and my village. In this moment, it was just her and I, my child's grandmother. I was confident that whatever she did, *had* to work. That was faith. It was in me to believe. She went to get a towel and told me to pull one end as she pulls the other. Minutes later, I had delivered a beautiful girl.

I remember the relief and joy I felt knowing that I had done it. I had delivered this baby and brought her forth. I knew then that was what I'd be doing the rest of my life, bringing her forth. I was unable to hold my child right after birth. My body was hemorrhaging. I remember holding my daughter hours later noticing a red mark on her back. I questioned it and was told it was her birth mark. Something in my spirit told me it wasn't the right answer and I wouldn't accept it. I didn't let it go. Even when I stopped asking questions, my spirit was unsettled.

As time passed on I noticed the spot never changed colors. Layers of skin started to come off but the color was still there and the mark was still evident. In my spirit I kept hearing cancer. A month after she was born, they saw pre-cancer cells on my cervix. At my appointment they informed me that they would remove half of my cervix and I wouldn't be able to have any more children. They told me it would be five to six years before it would grow back. After my appointment I called and told the father of my child while rushing to my mother's house to relay the news to her as well.

After talking it over with my mother, I decided to take a nap and rest. I had a dream that I was before a Priest and he was praying for healing and touching parts of my body. I was sure that I had a terminal illness. I woke up weeping and telling my mother about the dream before calling my doctor to tell them I needed to come in as soon as possible. I needed them to act on what I saw. We went in and they saw half of my cervix was white and covered in cancer. They said it was treatable and all they had to do was treat the cells and kill it before it escalated. Within a matter of weeks I was diagnosed with pre-cervical cancer and underwent immediate outpatient surgery. My doctors said I wouldn't have anymore kids, *especially* before my cervix grew back. As for the baby, they were able to rule out cancer. She had a rare condition of psoriasis that was hard to treat.

Despite what Doctors said exactly three years to the date of my surgery I found out I was pregnant again. There was an ice storm in Texas when I was driving down the road and got into a car accident. I went to the hospital to be examined because I was having severe stomach pain. During the exam they discovered that I was four months pregnant with my son. What they told me would take five years (as far as my cervix growing back) took only three years. God does what He wants and He does it well. The enemy fought me with both of my children. It was safe for me to understand that my children were chosen by God. As they grew up I was blessed to see the prophetic arise in both of my children yet in different ways. I began to equip and coach my kids. It was important to me to give them tools and understanding for their gift. Both of my children are dreamers and can see clear as day. I knew I had to pour and impart into them, much like my father did for me. The Lord showed me that when He is serious about a family, he will go through each generation until He gets the yes the Kingdom needs.

Chapter 2

The Daughter

I'll never forget when my dad came home and told my mother "I'm accepting the call to ministry." She respected his decision and he had no choice but to respect hers when she responded "Well, I'm not called to that so this probably won't work." My mother went to church, she was Baptist but she wasn't *in* church and she didn't have any desire or unction to be in the way she knew my father had just decided. Everything we knew as a family, had just changed. I had no idea that the decision my father made would now become a life of spotlight, gifting and ultimately a decision being made for me. My father wasn't just having a career change. My father was called to model Christ amongst the world and I had no idea what that truly meant for me.

Things began to quickly shift, and we weren't all shifting in the same direction. Our foundation as a family, was strong but we each had individual paths to walk down in order to become. My siblings and I had no idea that doing that as preachers kids would be much more difficult. I always remembered the standard my parents set before me but I had no idea the standard the world would now have for me. I had no idea anybody was expecting anything of Darilyn. I had no idea that because he decided, they expected me to decide instantaneously, too.

My father always spoke of the gift on my life. Since I was a little girl he was consistent in letting me know that I wasn't just made for "great" things but I was made for *God* things. I knew one day that would unfold but I never paid it much mind and I didn't know that I would have to walk in a level of consciousness in order to obtain an undeniable destiny. I expected to be much older before I decided to walk in the call on my life. In fact, I thought it was custom for people to expect me to be just like my father, after children and living my life to decide "it's time". I didn't get that same grace. Not only was God shifting my family but if people had their way, they wanted to shift me too, before I was ready to obey.

Many people, have no idea what it means to be a Pastors daughter. They see the outside of things, the "Glitz and Glam" of ministry if you will. Now that my father was a preacher and the world had their eyes on us, we no longer had the luxury of making mistakes without an audience. We were put in the limelight when we much rather have had the courtesy of figuring out who we were in the background. Though my parents did everything to ensure we lived a balanced life, the facts are things were different for us. I'd often have to consider the scripture *whom much is given, much is required.*

It was funny that while my father was serious about God and His business, I was serious about living my life. Don't get me wrong, I've always loved the Lord and been faithful to church. I just wasn't always surrendered to the transforming Power of Christ. I wanted all the things I never got to have. Yet while on a path to self-discovery my choices looked like destruction to many. I was young and I wanted the chance, to fall. I knew I was gifted. I knew my Father was a preacher. I knew I was anointed but I didn't know, who I was outside of that. I took the long way to become.

Suddenly there was a time in my life that surrendering didn't sound like a bad idea anymore. What I had on my "to do later" list, became a present priority. I was truly contemplating surrendering and walking this thing out. I knew God was calling me higher, and I had the perfect example in front of me on how to do it, my father. My dad placed a word over my head for years and he consistently affirmed it. That word became seed in the ground. He deposited something in me and suddenly he saw a return on that investment. My desire to be me changed, into a desire to be who the Lord called me to be. I was shifting. I finally got to a place of full surrender, but we all know that much like everyone else, it just doesn't start off that way. We say no before we say yes, just like most babies with their first words. There comes a time in your life when you're sitting in your mess and either you're shaking your head left to right in disapproval or your blatantly yelling "no" in full tantrum. Now that I had given God my yes, I wasn't okay with my yes being a duplicate or an echo of my father's.

I believe in legacy and I believe that I'm a part of his legacy and I will uphold and honor it when he's gone from this earth. However, there's a stigma on preacher kids when we say yes to ministry. People judge it from the same sense of our parents. I don't plan to be my father, though I am led by my father. I believe, and so does he, that the Lord has strategically and intentionally designed me and my ministry to be authentic yet still effective. There is such a strong pressure to duplicate my father's anointing that I now understand I don't have to yield to in order to honor and respect the call on his life.

I'll never forget when I began taking the call seriously. My mother was ill at the time and my Pastor gave us instructions to go and lay our hands on any sick loved ones we were believing God to heal following service. I went straight to my mother's house and did what I was told to do despite how she felt about me embracing ministry. Ever since I first began to walk out the call on my life, my mother had an interesting response. She had always been supportive of my endeavors but this was different for her. This was truly outside of her lane. When I would do certain things she would make remarks like "Is that how a woman of God acts?" She had her fair share of mocking me. She never flat out disapproved but she had a strong opinion that was very clear.

My mom felt like life was coming full circle because I was embracing ministry like my father knew I would. My mother saw my involvement in church but always felt like people in church were not serious. She lumped us all together. On top of that, my mother realized my taste in men had changed along with my desire to embrace my call. I have dated two Bishops in my life. When she found out she asked me "Darilyn, do you really want to do this? This position isn't for the weak." My mother knew what came with being with a man of the collar. She didn't want me to be oblivious. She encouraged me to get close to God and to guard myself. She knew what I was up against.

I didn't go chasing Pastors, they approached me. Once again, my calling was coming after me.

On the other hand, my father was excited that I was going down a path similar to his own. He had always encouraged me to pursue a righteous man, he just had no idea it would be Bishops and Pastors. That was a plus! It was befitting. Though he encouraged this, he had no idea how much church and leadership had changed since he was young.

At least 90% of men would say I'm different and hard. In other words I play no games. The silent woman that went along with anything just to say I was with a man of influence wasn't me. I was okay with dating a Pastor, I wasn't okay with being something I wasn't. One thing I learned quickly was, everyone was not my father. Every Prophet and Preacher weren't the example I had before me. I had no idea how broken men of the collar were.

So many are actually broken and show up functionally, so you can't identify the brokenness from afar. I would tell my father the things I came to know, leaving him stunned. Most Pastors cannot balance family and church, and that's never been my father's life! And please do not get me started on their sexual appetite. All in all, these men were a trip and I was sure to let my dad know!

Later down the line during my spiritual development, my father placed me in the hands of another ministry. His friend of forty years was to become my Pastor. My father ministered out of another city and could no longer shepherd me the way he sought out to so he sent me to a trusted voice in the city in order to be cultivated. Though my father was an example, he was no longer my covering. My father sent me to a prophetic house knowing that I had a gift of prophecy on my life. His decision to send me to this church was best for my development and apart of Gods plan.

Against my father's better judgment and what the Lord said, I left my church home prematurely after being there for many years. I was being cultivated and taught like I knew I needed to be but I was hurt. My Pastor trained me in such a way that I was grateful for and we had no issues. However when he was away from home on assignment, I had an interaction that left a bad taste in my mouth. Being wounded by another leader in the ministry caused me to leave. I made a hasty and emotional decision. This particular leader and I had a working relationship and I felt mishandled in an interaction between the two of us. She was a woman who believed in mentorship, and I simply was not her mentee. We viewed our dynamic from two different perspectives which meant we approved of two different types of communication between the two of us and the lines became blurred. I wasn't happy with this interaction and I left. We didn't see eye to eye and that was it for me.

Time went on and I knew I made a mistake, not by standing up for me but not seeing the bigger picture. I knew that I was called to the church I was attending. I knew my Pastors were who I needed and I never questioned that. As a devoted member and even as someone in Ministry and Leadership, I knew better than to become unplanted due to an outside situation. When my father sent me to my home church, he saw something in my leader that he had to deposit into me and he was right. I later not only reconciled with this leader who hurt me, but I reconciled with my Pastors and returned home. It was important for me to remember where I belonged.

Apart of realizing you are Her is knowing who needs to be around you, who needs to shepherd you and controlling your emotions for the sake of sustaining yourself in every way. I had too much at stake to forfeit spiritual sustainability and disobey Gods instruction. Too often we let people, emotions and other fickle things dictate where we stand and how. I had enough of that. I was dedicated to me, and that meant being dedicated to everything and everyone good for me. Being planted allows you to be accountable and accounted for. Ladies, being planted isn't just something you do when it is convenient but something you do when you are called, mature and

HER.

Chapter 3

The Spirit That Wants

Girlfriend, here's your moment of truth.

Sisterhood is indeed a necessity and not a want. I know in this day and time there's women out there who want to convince you that they stand alone and don't need anyone, but it's a lie. In fact, as a Christian the Bible shows us countless times why we *need* community. True and authentic sisterhood is a benefit. I've been blessed to be a friend and to be befriended by some incredible women. However, that didn't exempt me from running into a few snakes in the grass. Even as one who is anointed, gifted and discerning, sometimes I too didn't see what was in front of me.

Beyond a benefit, sisterhood is often a mirror. The perspective of your life, should be a reflection of who you're surrounded by. Let that sink in. With that being said, in every stage of my life I've had to look back on what my friendships said about where I was. Sometimes, the confirmation I needed was in the friendships I did the most pouring into. Sometimes, all the warning I needed, was in the friends who shouldn't have been so up close. Sisterhood, is a step further than community, it's a bond between two women that are so close they decide, they are family. When you are family, you have the same DNA be it natural, spiritual or even emotional. Somehow, someway, y'all are connected by something deeper than shopping and gossip. In today's time, when we see something about a friend we don't like we need to check ourselves and then check the connection immediately after. We aren't in a time where we can afford to be bamboozled by assassins posing as friends. Wolves are in sheep's clothing and the only way we will know, is sharpening our discernment.

In a time where betrayal has become second nature to some, many are disconnecting from community in an attempt to guard themselves, but the truth is completely disconnecting from people means doing ourselves a disservice. The only way we can truly protect ourselves, is to fast, pray and *watch*. In Matthew 26:41, it tells us to pray and watch and many of us have stopped at prayer. In 2021, I was living life a bit different from the one I'm living today. I was happy. I was content. I was good. It was 6am in the morning when a friend of mine called me and told me "Sis, watch the women around you. One of them is about to betray you in the worst way." This is why we can't do life alone while walking out the call. There are sisters in your corner who are watching when you're only praying and praying when you're only watching. The thing about real covenant relationships and people tied to your purpose, they see what you don't.

There are people on your left that the people on your right are side eyeing because something about them just doesn't sit well with their spirit. The thing about this is, we have to be willing to listen to the people in our corner. We have to know when they hear God for us and honor the gifts of The Spirit. Not even a month later, that 6am word was manifested. I found out that a friend of mine, was sleeping with my then boyfriend. It didn't take a Prophet calling out my address or spelling out my name. It took a friend assigned to me and my life who truly covers me to hear God and act on what she heard, immediately. It matters who you call sister. If you can't listen to what they have to say, it's not a sister. If you can't trust them in totality, you need to be watchful. Sisters need accountability amongst one another in order to truly be family. No accountability and no trust leave room for much error.

In one weekend I found out a whole year of information. Forgiveness wasn't an option in my book. I had found out someone I called a friend, wanted my entire life, my man included. She wanted it so bad that she even told him about me cheating with a man that was going through a divorce. The stage was now set. When I decided to cheat on my man I was already four years into the relationship. I was needing something my current man wasn't providing. Our relationship was dying and the man I cheated with made me feel alive. His love was passionate, loving, safe, and made me feel free. Our connection was one for the movies but in reality he was only my side piece. He was the fix when the oil was low. Things took a turn when he told me he was in love with me. I knew I needed a Plan B because my situation didn't allow me to pursue anything serious.

While trying to figure out my next I discovered that an associate was going on dates with my man as well! The crazy part about it both my friend and associate were in cahoots! They both made a bet to see who would sleep with the man first. Not to mention text messages of them asking him to leave me. The betrayal was real. These were two women who claimed to be in happy relationships. How did this happen? How well do we really know our circle of friends? Can you imagine a woman eating at your house, but the whole time plotting to take your life? A woman feeling like she will be a better fit than you? My decision was easy to make.

Some of our mutual friends began to play both sides. Ladies watch women who remain friends with women who betray you in the worst way. A side will always have to be picked, and if not they will play both sides until it blows up. The first "friend" of mine that slept with my man ended up trying to commit suicide. The guilt was getting the best of her. This woman believed that I was speaking negatively of her and quickly found out that wasn't the case. Her actions changed the course of her own life without her considering it, especially relationally. Some of our mutual friends started to exclude her from gatherings and more. Many would speak to her if they crossed paths while to others this was fake, those people simply cut her off. Not long after that the man exposed both women he slept with. Both of these women had been in my house and to several events I had hosted. They all began turning on one another and feeding me information- the man, the friend and the associate. The friend of mine didn't have much to say but the associate came to me directly in an attempt to move past this. It was interesting that the associate wanted to deal with it at the root vs. my own friend.

The truth about both the man and the women came to the forefront. The associate was shocked to find out that not only did the women come forward, but the man did too. He was honest when I brought the information to him and let me know exactly what it was. He began showing receipts of what the encounters actually portrayed way beyond the information given to me from the women. Where I thought he was the aggressor, I quickly found out everyone played a part. This exposure even opened up space for conversation on a deeper level between him and I. Even when we didn't work out, it opened space to address some wounds and for closure to move on peacefully. At the time we were staying together, but after this I knew it was time to not only move on but *out*.

Things started to get crazy around my thirty-ninth birthday. Life was happening while I was still distracted by current situations. From 2021-2023 I was working two jobs. Money was good and I had over twelve-thousand dollars a month coming in. Unexpectedly, in June of 2023 I had two weeks to decide if I was going to stay with my long term company. I decided to stay only to get laid off two months later. Suddenly, the solid ground underneath me became shaky. At that point, it had been one transition after the other. I was going through it in what seemed like every way possible. I left my current relationship, moved out overnight, and spent six thousand dollars on new furniture and ten months into the new lease I was evicted. Due to losing my job and awaiting unemployment, I didn't have it. I was hurt in more ways than one, now I wanted all parties to really suffer. I didn't deserve any of this, that much I *knew*!

Many asked how was I able to forgive the man but not the women involved. Let's discuss my process of forgiveness:

1. Apology to SELF.
2. Acknowledge what you allowed.
3. Acknowledge how you contributed.
4. Address your man.
5. Deal with the elephant in the room no matter how long it takes.
6. Identify your trigger points.
7. Wait until you are clear to reconcile.
8. Deal with the layers of wounds that seem not to heal.
9. Identify and find you.

10. Finally, have a grown woman conversation.

The math was simple, I left the door open for reconciliation from an honest and mature standpoint and he abided. Not all parties were willing to fully engage their truths in the conversations needed for closure and co-existing. Every last woman that betrayed me came back to ask for forgiveness and to reconcile. I actually couldn't believe it! It shocked many of us as well. But God has a funny way of spinning the block after testing. Forgiveness wasn't an option. After deep diving within myself and having multiple conversations I realized there was just no room to reconcile with both women.

I wanted them to suffer. It wasn't so much because they slept with my man. It was the deception and manipulation that went on for years. See, it typically isn't the act we don't heal from but it's the betrayal that takes longer. When I turned forty years old something broke off of me. Out of nowhere my past didn't exist. I was moving in another phase of grace. When I say I was on cloud nine, I mean it. God was gutting me from the inside out. God was checking my motives and my heart because the anger of betrayal was still surfacing. He got me together. I was no longer going to allow this season or betrayal to consume me. It was in the past.

I decided to turn pain into success and money. I went back to school to finish my degree in Healthcare Administration and obtained my coding certification. Oh, I was in my vein! God saw it as the perfect time to test my faith. I ended up having to move back to the same house I left with this man. Yes, girlfriend I moved back. Now I was forced to face all the elephants in the room. I was forced to stay instead of pack up. What helped me and the man to move forward was honesty. A mature and grown conversation regarding why we *both* did things. I had my cross to bear and my sins to answer for as well. Beyond that, I still hadn't forgiven or talked to my old friend. I had to deal with this cheating spirit that kept running in and out of my relationship and that was the priority as long as him and I were together.

Ladies never second guess yourself. We live in a day and time where women don't understand sisterhood. Instead women are in competition with the little girl within them that never grew up to be a woman. As women we have to change how the world views women. In order to change this we have to start from within and be that change. Ladies as you advance in business, ministry and your career it's important to examine your circle one more time. I've learned to watch the quiet ones, and the ones that don't have many friends.

As a woman your desires relationally, physically, and spiritually should push you to higher heights. It's better to reconcile than to expose. It's better to communicate than to die with unpacked baggage. Women of maturity and status have conversations that lead to a resolution. Whatever you survive helps to builds you up. If you want closure forgive *you* first for what you allowed. In order to leave an impact, you must know what it is like to both forgive and survive.

Chapter Four

The Impact

In life every woman desires to be loved properly. By nature as a woman one of our strengths is to impact and take people or things under our wing. Healthy love and sex matters. There comes a point in every woman's life when you must examine your impact. How do you contribute to your own life? How do you *impact* those around you? When it comes to men why do you continue to date the same spirit but in a different body?

I believe that my taste and selection of men have been quite interesting over time. My taste in men has always depended on what season of my life I was in. If I was in my fun season, I desired a man that matched that. If I was in a season of growth, I desired a man that matched that. Yet, in every season I desired a man that could balance me out physically, mentally, and emotionally. I often explain to people that maturity while parenting is having a healthy co-parent relationship but also being a healthy *you*. Developing a healthy co-parenting relationship first starts with being realistic and in alignment. We had to realize this partnership is not temporary, but permanent and that alone shifts how you co-exist. Respect centers reality.

In October 2017 my life took an interesting turn relationship wise. I met a man who wasn't really my type but he was a cool person overall. I gave him a chance and he really grew on me. What I once didn't like, I now did. He wasn't my type originally because he was what I considered over the top. He was a well-rounded man open to life on a whole new level. He was a brother, friend, and a *grown* man. He could shift any environment and I loved that about him. I knew I had found a rider with no questions asked. Little did I know, how well rounded he was would be costly. There were no boundaries and things took a turn.

Long nights and conversations turned into five years of physical, mental, and spiritual growth and long hours of tears. This relationship tested every part of my life. It provoked me as a woman, sister, daughter and mother. This relationship could've had me serving five to ten in prison. All of the years of verbal abuse and betrayal got the best of me.

I knew one year into the relationship I was in for a ride. Yet, I chose to remember the solid friendship we had. It wasn't enough in the end.

The relationship became so toxic this man would invite women over to gatherings and claim they were friends but I knew better. I remember feeling as though the relationship was leading me to a road of orange jumpsuits. I recall his ex-girlfriend sent an edible arrangement to the house we shared on Valentine's Day one year. The card read, "Meet me for dinner later." I knew in this moment without a doubt this wasn't just another woman but he had some baggage and possibly a stronghold that had never been identified. Often times when relationships end the woman always blames another woman for her pain. I found myself in this position. I was completely caught off guard as the other woman who knew nothing about the previous woman.

As time went on that same woman found me on Facebook. She was convinced that I knew who she was because they had previously been together seventeen years. I made a post of a photo of him in my house on Facebook when a mutual friend of hers saw it and sent the post to her. She sought me out as a friend on Facebook and immediately began to indirectly spill the tea. I asked him who she was because I knew something was up. He affirmed what I knew. As time went on she came out of the shadows, put a stop to the subliminal post and emailed me all of this tea! She decided to tell me all of these things concerning him that I didn't know. I was the new woman on the block but she was the seasoned woman who was able to see him through every season. Imagine keeping the new woman informed about a man you still desire to spend your life with.

I was informed to watch any woman he called sister or home girl. Apparently it was code for side piece. The plot twist, it was all true. Ladies your gut never lies. So many of these things I suspected but couldn't prove and finally I no longer had to wonder. One thing about a bitter woman she will tell you everything you need to know and more. I use to say to myself, *Darilyn you are not a nurse. Explain why you continue to take on patient after patient!?* The fact is, I was dating the same spirit but in a different body.

When I look back on the five serious relationships I had in life, I see so much. *Yes*! I have only been in five serious relationships in my whole life. At age forty-one I look back on past relationships and immediately say "never again" but I know that each one was attached to different areas of my purpose. Here's where we have to separate the assignment from purpose. We are not purposed to be with everyone. Some people are our assignment. My relationship of five years broke me and allowed me to grow all at the same time. That is typically how it goes, what breaks you down will grow you up! The independent woman in me was like *girl are you crazy?!? RUN!* I have always had a great relationship with both fathers of my children. It was to the point I would vent to them about my romantic relationships. In time we had grown to be more than just co-parents but friends. One day one of them called me and said "DARILYN WAKE UP. This isn't you! Girl let it go."

It was at the moment I knew I was in too deep. I sobered up, quickly. I knew I had to make a decision to reconcile, fight, or catch the next flight. As I replayed years of wasted time with not one but now three men. I said to myself once again "Darilyn you are not a nurse. Why are you accepting patients!?" It seemed like every man I crossed had some sort of issue I thought I could fix. Outside of their flaws and their wrongs, I played a role too. At this moment I had to take a look at myself. It was much more than the betrayal and all the cheating, it was now up to me and what I was willing to deal with. I was on a rollercoaster of actions, reactions and blame. And the one thing I was consistently losing in all of that was, time. Did I want my long-term relationship or did I now want to fully pursue this man I was cheating with? What was it about me that hadn't fully moved on?

I had to understand my natural ability to give and help had me bound to thinking I couldn't drop people, even if that boundary was necessary. I finally realized the most important person to not drop was Darilyn. I went through an entire season of mentally transitioning out of a relationship I was still physically in. Everyday was a fight for my mental and a fight to move forward. I faced this all while encouraging and praying for others. Finally something clicked for me. What I was once only doing mentally, now turned into physical momentum.

I still recall the incident that caused me to move suddenly. I was plotting and planning to leave and not look back. The crazy part about it some people in his circle helped me in the process. I cleaned a whole house out in two hours and was in a new one as if I lived there for years. Ladies, we all know that in our process to pursuing more and letting go of settling we first leave mentally. It is nothing wrong with taking the time to process mentally and emotionally before hitting the ground running. It is only a problem when you don't put your thoughts into action. As a woman we are sometimes taught to choose everything but us. Kids, career, man, misery, business, friends etc and then us. Everything we do starts with us, and if we don't pursue wholeness every decision that comes from us will showcase bad fruit and brokenness. And we all know fruit, is the sign of the tree it came from.

Chapter 5

Breech But Ready

There comes a moment in every woman's life where you must have a full term delivery by any means necessary. Most women hear that and assume birthing a real life baby, but I'm speaking in terms of purpose! Too often as women, we put down purpose to pick up "busy". We pick up relationships, career, our savior complex and everything else that causes a delay in our delivery process. When we pick up anything that isn't meant for us as we are pursuing purpose it leads to complications in the birthing process. It leads to a breech delivery.

A breech birth is when a baby is born bottom first instead of head first like normal. Around 3–5% of pregnant women at term have a breech baby. Due to their higher than average rate of possible complications for the baby, breech births are generally considered higher risk. This woman is finally about to push out the baby, the purpose, she's been waiting for and now she has to worry about being high risk. High risk for pain. High risk for inconvenience. High risk for failure of successful delivery. High risk for disappointment.

After walking through many different chapters in life my purpose was no longer coming out head first. It was now coming out feet first. Spiritually and naturally I was getting ready to deliver a full term baby breech. I was breech but ready. I had accepted my current condition but I was ready for labor anyway! It was year 2023 going into 2024 when life shifted for the better, so I *thought*. Imagine dating a man of the cloth, again! Him and I clicked instantly and we even thought alike. But I realized early on, I was once again being a nurse. I didn't just have a man but I had a patient who needed reassurance and needed help pushing. My patient needed a reason to live again.

Just when I thought it was time for me to give birth, I realized I was on assignment once again. During this assignment, it really hit me that you have to be built for it to date a man of the cloth. I saw what it looks like up close but I now knew the weight of what it cost to truly be with a man of the collar. Believe it or not they are the most down to earth men you will ever meet. As women we believe that dating a man of the cloth helps to birth us out into purpose and/or ministry. When in reality there are very few who will provoke and push the gift their woman carries. As a woman in ministry I looked forward to me and my partner pouring into one another in that way. It didn't dawn on me that in this case, my partner would *be* my assignment vs. taking on assignments with me.

Here I was, in a favorable season yet high risk. I was doing the work and finally on my way to birthing more purpose when I found myself, breech. To go further I realized I had become an increased risk to self. *What does it mean to be an increased risk to self?* An increased risk is a breach in security. You are now a threat to everyone you come in contact with. As a woman I've been pregnant before, both naturally and figuratively. I was sure I had this under control! I quickly realized what I once was prepared to do on my own, I now needed help. It was going to take a team to assist me with a full term pregnancy. I was now Elizabeth looking for Mary. When you're breech, you typically are in a mix of two seasons.

Two emotions fill a woman with a breech pregnancy, anxiety *AND* joy. When you are birthing purpose, breech, you find your residue of your last season mixing into your new seasons excitement. It is essential to have a Midwife to keep you focused and grounded. I was carrying twins, with no midwife. I was exhausted and excited but determined for purpose to be fulfilled nonetheless.

At this point, everything seemed to be coming up. I had past relationships reaching out to reconcile. God began dealing with those who wronged me. During month nine I couldn't understand how I was birthing a book, finishing my degree, eliminating strongholds relationships, to now having reconciliation sessions with individuals who sabotaged my name. I was forgiving others during a season of uncertainty. I had the faith and maturity for both. I realized, I couldn't have one without the other. The closer I got to delivery, the more there was to do, heal from and become. So much of this was new, I needed a Mary to help me deliver this baby.

Though life was in alignment with my future, the past was coming up. I began to prepare to give birth to everything I once sat aside. Right in the midst of my momentum my past began to ask for forgiveness. Not just one or two but three past relationships were seeking reconciliation. Do I keep moving forward or revisit? Though I began reconciling I wasn't naive enough to not continue to be careful of who I let into my delivery room. In order to have a stress free delivery, who is in the room matters. When you are already high risk, you want to make sure who is present won't be a threat to your delivery. It's important you have the right individuals to see you through. It takes certified help to assist with birthing. Not only did I find my midwives but I began embracing the community assigned to me. This community is the village who will see my babies grow over time.

It is something about giving birth regardless of the diagnosis. When God realized I was committed and surrendered beyond the circumstances the game changed. Heaven began backing me up and that simple fact gave me the stamina to continue forward. God began blessing my sacrifice right before my eyes. I walked into fullness in every area of my life. My heart became filled to the brim with gratitude for the now and the next. It was abundantly clear that the purpose being birthed was about to exceed my expectations just like the word declares. Even in delivery, God sent several words to confirm what He ordained. Every labor pain suddenly became worth it. In the midst of writing what I thought would be the last chapter of my book, the Lord pulled on me to produce more and then my physical body went under attack, right smack dap in the middle of my delivery. That attack wanted everything in me to forfeit my purpose but it had no idea that I was committed to the process. I was positioned to give birth and it was no turning back for me. I had midwives pushing me from a distance. Heaven had already spoken. I began to confess "I shall live and not die and as long as I have breath, I'm doing what He called me to." I don't know what woman needs to hear this but keep pushing, your baby shall come forth. Purpose shall live in you. You are built to become. Deliver!

Chapter 6

Her Prayer

There comes a time in every it girls life that
we have to realize that you cannot be HER on your
own. When the weight of the world, the worry of if
you are doing enough, the stench of betrayal and
all the business of the roles you play become too
much and you finally realize, you are tired. It is all
exhausting and you need one designated place to
rest. When I say rest, I don't mean a nap. I don't
mean the kind of sleep where your mind never
turns off and you toss and turn all night. But I
mean, the kind of rest you get when you truly lean
into Jesus.

I remember a time I closed my eyes with no intent to pray but I just couldn't stand to look at anything any longer. I couldn't look at the piles of laundry, my phone or myself. And suddenly that moment that wasn't intended for prayer felt like the best time to speak to God. I opened my mouth and said "God, I don't know how to say this right now. I am not trying to impress you. I'm just tired. Tired of feeling stuck. Tired of wondering if I am ever going to become who you made me to be." I went on to tell God all of my worries and concerns. I told him "I want to live on purpose. I want to do what I'm called to, even though I have no idea what that looks like. Can you close doors that drain me and open new ones? I want love; real, soft and safe love. I want someone I can trust. I want something that is grounded and good for the me I'm called to be. I want to heal. I want to heal from every part of me that aches. I want to heal from the things I can't speak out-loud. Lord, I want all of this to be successful. *I* want to be successful, and not in the way the world talks about but in the way that you approve of. I want to make an impact, a difference." When I stopped praying my whole life didn't change in an instant but something was certainly different. I felt His presence and I sat to listen. I knew He was there and since He was there I wanted Him to have the floor in case He was to say anything back. "The promise is still good." He said and my spirit settled immediately. There was the peace my soul was begging for. There was the word I needed to hold on to.

Ladies, you will have tough seasons. Some days you will be so worn down by the weight of it all and you'll feel as if you have no strength to stand. Some days the grief of disappointment will consume you. Other days, you will feel on top of the world. You will smile brightly with no assistance. Regardless of what you face, you will always need Him to face it with you. Regardless of what is in front of you or behind you, being grounded by building a consistent prayer life is the key to building anything else in your life. Your faith is the foundation. And the strength of your faith comes from your commitment to prayer. For the next several pages, consume your heart with the prayers provided.

Her Prayer

Heavenly Father, we thank You because You are the answer to all things. Lord, we thank You for the activity of our limbs. We thank You now for being the beginning and end of all things, Lord. We thank You for safe arrivals and departures. Lord, we thank You for a fresh wind of peace and clarity. We thank You for positioning and repositioning us for such a moment as this. Establish us in this hour so that we may soar above obstacles and delays. Now, Lord, anoint us for every assignment this week. May You get the glory this week, as many of us stand before people. We rebuke the strong man (him/her) that watches from afar, awaiting the opportunity to do the unthinkable. We cast down pride even now Father. May every spirit of pride come subject to your will and way. Lord arrest every spirit of pride regardless of title and or influence. Lord, there's an undeniable peace resting in the air even now. Today is full of miracles. I sense a strong need of reconciliation coming forth. You are calling many back to the place of readiness. You spoke and stated that now is the time to go. May You connect and send Your people to places and people they are called to. No more wasted time. Last but not least, send the wind!

In Jesus name, amen.

Her Prayer

"No Wasted Time, Nor Delay."

Heavenly Father, we come boldly to You to simply say thank You. Thank You for your life lessons and favors. Thank You for redeeming the time. Thank You for showing us now instead of later. Thank You for positioning one to pick up where another failed. We decree and declare that we aren't employees to time. But that "time" is an employee of ours. Lord, teach us how to manage and love properly. Lord, don't let Your people forfeit what's needed for "next." Thank You for strengthening eyesight and vision. We thank You for a temporary moment, but a bounce back anointing. Thank You for standards and secured boundaries. Lord, touch the minds of those struggling mentally. We come against every voice of opposition and confusion. We come against the spirit that watches from afar. We speak to every spirit of doubt that wrestles against itself Lord. Lord, we ask that You touch every woman that may come across this prayer. We interrupt plans of the enemy. We speak to the mental, physical, and emotional state of every woman and man suffering from depression and oppression. We speak to every negative thought and the need to retaliate against others. Touch every man who is struggling with the "what if" thoughts. Deal with the heart of "delay", Lord. Uproot the mindset of "wait" or "not yet.". Lord, touch the minds of leaders of any area who are functioning empty. Lord, touch the minds of those who keep going but never stop to see themselves. Lord, touch the bodies of leaders who look fine in public but are dying in private. We speak to the hearts of every leader who continues to miss their season, Lord. We decree and declare that, Lord, You do the revealing, shaking, and promoting. Lord, send Your people, people who understand the meaning of time. Lord, help Your people understand the importance of God connections. Lord, teach Your people how to manage and not fumble. Last but not least, Lord, empower Your people for "NEXT." Lord I thank You that I hear You saying "Prepare. You are getting ready to assist with a vision bigger than you."

In Jesus name, amen.

Her Prayer

I heard God say to tell His people, "God's accountability isn't like man's accountability. Know when I'm talking to you for you." Heavenly Father, we thank You for the ability to discern. We thank You for the ability to think clearly and freely. We thank You for good health and well-positioned posture. Lord, forgive us for the sins we have committed. Lord, we thank You for saving us from ourselves in this hour. We thank You for continuing to love us even when we doubt You. We thank You for seasons of warfare and trauma. We thank You for correcting us when we saw others but didn't see ourselves. We thank You for teachable seasons, places, and people. We thank You for undeniable growth during seasons of immaturity. Now Lord, we ask today that You walk the grounds of homes, workplaces etc. May You visit those who have been a blessing to others. May You decrease the strong man that sees fit to put himself or herself above others. Lord may You deal with the pride of hurt. May You blow on hearts and souls. May a strong conviction hit churches on Sunday from the pulpit to the very foundation of the structure. Send a mighty wind this weekend. May the saved, unsaved, and unsure experience God appointed moments this weekend. God may You raise up another. May You teach Your people the difference between accountability and responsibility. May You teach Your people from the pulpit to the grounds the difference between a spirit and self inflicted attacks. Lord increase our discernment. Deal with Your people's emotional states. Save every watching and monitoring spirit. Whew Lord, put Your people back together. Deal with the double minded leader and person. Deal with the cloudy minds now Father. Now Lord, we thank You. Last but not least let us be disciplined in our delivery but true to what we believe. In Jesus name, Amen.

Her Prayer

Abba, I honor You for being Lord God Yahweh. I honor You for being Lord Jesus Christ. I honor You for being the Comforter, the Holy Spirit. Lord, for such a time as this, wherever and whenever my sisters come across this prayer, and wherever they may be in life, I lift them up. I lift up my sisters who will come across this prayer, that they will receive everything they need from You. May their hearts' desires align with Your word. May they seek the Kingdom of Heaven before making any decisions regarding any area of their lives, according to Matthew 6:33. When the hardships of life come their way, help my sisters to seek You in their singleness, in their marriages, in motherhood, in their careers, and in their purpose. Help them not to seek things in the world to fulfill the flesh but to die to their flesh daily.

May they know that every plan You have for them is peace, not evil, and to give them an expected end (Jeremiah 29:11). I pray that my sisters will receive salvation, that they will become healed, delivered, set free, and filled with the Holy Spirit of Jesus Christ. May they always know and remember that You are with them and will never leave nor forsake them. Remind my sisters to remain strong in You and in the power of Your might. Remind my sisters that they are more than conquerors in Jesus Christ. Remind my sisters that no weapon formed against them will prosper. Remind my sisters to wear the full armor of God daily.

Remind my sisters that they are the head and not the tail. Remind them that they are lenders and not borrowers. Remind my sisters that they are fearfully and wonderfully made. Remind my sisters that they will not fail, for You are with them. Remind my sisters to kneel when they can't stand. Remind my sisters that they are a reflection of You. Remind my sisters that they are HER! In Jesus Christ's name, Amen.

Your I Am HER sister,
Relaina Warren

Her Prayer

Our God, our father, we Bless your Holy name on this day. You are the creator of all things we exalt and magnify your name. We thank You for Your compassion towards us for Your mercies are new every morning. Great is your faithfulness towards us. We thank You for the greatest gift You can give to us and that is our Lord and Savior Jesus Christ.

Now Lord we pray for Her. We pray for the woman, the wife, the mother and the daughter. We ask oh Father that You continue to build the total woman. We ask God that You would mend and heal her heart, her mind and soul. I pray God that You will give Her peace in her mind. I ask God that You would anoint her to continue to be a pitcher, full of water that pours into other women and people of all walks of life. Lord continue to allow her to thrive in this life that You have given to Her. Honor her for all that her hands have done and let her works bring her praise at the city gate. Lord we ask these things in the mighty name of Jesus Christ. In Jesus name, Amen.

Pastor Philip Walter

Her Prayer

Father in the name of Jesus, strengthen the person reading this. Help her to know that she is enough and that she has everything on the inside of her to finish. I bind fear off of the life of who may be reading this prayer. Fear is "False Evidence Appearing Real" and has no place in the Kingdom. I bind generational choices and curses going back thirty generations. I bind all blood line curses in Jesus Mighty Name. I loose the Freedom of God to flow in your life. I pray that you believe there is nothing you have done that will stop God from loving you. I pray that you remember 1 John 1:9 (NIV) If we confess our sins, He is faithful and just and will forgive us of our sins and purify us from all unrighteousness. Lord cover Your daughter and protect her from danger seen and unseen. I pray Psalms 91 over you. God, I pray that you nullify and dismantle any ungodly soul ties. Disconnect her from people who have ulterior motives. As she gets more into Your word Father, open up her spiritual eyes and ears. God heighten her spiritual discernment and awareness. Father, strengthen her for the Journey ahead. In Jesus Name, Amen.

Speak these daily affirmations over yourself:
I am complete in Him. (Colossians 2:10)
I am Strong in the Lord. (Ephesians 6:10)
I am a New Creature in Christ. (2 Corinthians 5:17)
I am more than a Conqueror. (Romans 8:37)
I am Free from Condemnation. (John 5:24)
I am Healed By the stripes of Jesus. (1Peter 2:25 and Isaiah 53:6)

Cheree Brooks

Chapter 7

After all I had been through, all I had done and all I had seen I was okay with my truth. However, I understood my truth and reality didn't have to stay the same. I understood that my mental state could shift my truth, by embracing hard decisions. I was one step away from a complete shift. All I had to do was make up in my mind, that I wanted different and different would follow. I was in position for breakthrough.

   I realized that my previous seasons changed some core realities about me but it did not change my DNA. All I had to do was return to self, and to God completely and my true DNA would reveal that my last season was just that, merely a season. I had to make this next chapter a personal one so I could really get back to me and the promises of God concerning me. There's no way to truly face the chapters of your life, without first diagnosing every season of your life. I diagnosed my seasons. I understood why they were necessary and then I understood why the next season was mandatory to be "the return". I was determined not to let it all go in vain. I knew giving birth meant transparency. What was once my struggle was to now be a road map for the next woman to identify as HER. I knew there were people who were to read my story and choose to live.

The return is inevitable for each person who ever got sidetracked while on their way to promise. The return is biblical. The prodigal son was distracted by his own ambitions and he wanted to rush the process. He wanted to enjoy his inheritance before time. He was distracted by his desires when he should have been focused on his DNA that would soon give him his inheritance, much like us. If you have had seasons of distraction, turmoil and "If it ain't one thing it's another" that is how you know your season of the return isn't near it is *here!* When it is time for a return, no demon in hell can stop it.

The return is overcoming what could and should've killed you. It is about self-forgiveness for what you allowed. The return is the power to love anyway. It is walking the other woman through terminal illness knowing you have one man in common. The return is the power of forgiveness. It is when their negative opinions and lies create a platform that is designed just for you.

The return is realizing that your healing starts with a personal decision.

You cannot embrace the return without dealing with your own prognosis. Here's where you deal with the diagnosis and prognosis of your life. When it's personal there's no blaming. It's the growth of reality you feed off of. It's the power to preserve your pour. Your pour consist of all that is on the inside of you. There comes a moment when you have to stop giving yourself away to everybody and save something for yourself. Embrace the original you, the you that got detoured while focused. It's like having a GPS on audibly feeding you directions, yet you still go right instead of left.

Like the prodigal son, we wandered. We tasted the poison of the world and called it wine.

We traded our crowns for crumbs, until we realized we were worth so much more. Our decisions caused us to silence the voice that use to roar with purpose but just like him we came to ourselves. We came to ourselves in the mud, in the mess, and in the middle of what looked like the end. That's the beauty of the return, it doesn't begin in perfection it begins in awakening. Awakening to the fact that we have to heal, to return. I came back dirty. I came back bruised but I came back, not only to God but to *me.* Sis, this is the moment you return to all things you. This is the moment you dive into the inner you and deal with all that is broken. This isn't the moment for blame, but the moment to balance what's not stable. This is the moment you realize that every detour was seen and still, God chose you.

I'm HER. Her who got distracted. Her who overcame adversity. I'm Her who returned. I returned to self. I returned to my church. I returned to my true DNA. My return required me to realign. My return required me to realign—realign my purpose, my focus, and my environment. I had to let go of what was familiar but no longer fruitful. I had to confront the parts of me that were still addicted to distraction and call myself back into divine order. It wasn't easy. It was raw, it was humbling, but it was surrendered and sacrificial. That realignment placed me in a position to fully embrace the return—not just as a moment, but as a movement. I no longer live in fragments. I no longer apologize for who I am in God. I am whole. I am found. I am home. And let me be clear; I'm not just passing through this time. I'm here to stay —rooted, restored, and ready to help other women come back to themselves too.

About The Author

Darilyn Johnson is a mom, woman of God, and entrepreneur. She is a woman who wears many hats and whatever she sets out in her heart to do, she does in full excellence. She firmly believes in her favorite quote "Finish what you start!". This keeps her motivated to continue full force in all that God has set out for her to do. Beyond being on the go in business and ministry Darilyn enjoys travel for leisure! When she isn't traveling you can find her having a self care day filled with refueling and full glamour. She finds passion in being a resource to others and helping people to be successful in whatever their endeavor may be. As Darilyn fully embraces what it means to be an Author and all of the new territory attached to it, you can expect to see her around the globe pushing this book to ladies everywhere! Please keep up with the Author at Darilynjohnson.com.

Made in United States
Orlando, FL
12 June 2025

62038955R00059